Crossing Borders

Stories of Immigrants

By Thomas Lang

CELEBRATION PRESS
Pearson Learning Group

Contents

Coming to America

For hundreds of years, people have left their homes in other countries to make new lives in the United States. These people are called **immigrants**. Each year, hundreds of thousands of new immigrants arrive in the United States.

They come for many reasons. Some are escaping governments that treat them badly. Others are looking for better jobs and new opportunities. Some people just want to live somewhere new.

The three people in this book are all immigrants. Margarita, Hector, and Marilyn all came to the United States to make new and better lives for themselves. Each has a different story to tell.

Margarita Rozenfeld moved from Ukraine when she was twelve.

Hector Grillone moved from Argentina when he was six.

Marilyn Chin moved from Hong Kong when she was nine.

Margarita Rozenfeld

Imagine living in a country where you were unfairly treated because of your religion. **Discrimination** was part of life for Margarita Rozenfeld and her family. They were Jewish and lived in Kiev, the capital of Ukraine. Jews living in Ukraine were often denied opportunities like good jobs and good educations.

Margarita's parents decided that they didn't want to raise Margarita in Ukraine. "My parents were afraid that I wouldn't have any opportunities," Margarita says. In 1989, when Margarita was twelve, they left Ukraine to make a new life in the United States.

It was a difficult move for Margarita. She liked her life in Ukraine, and she was afraid to go to America. "I guess I was just really sad that I had to leave everything behind," she says. The Rozenfelds had to leave family, friends, and most of their **possessions** behind.

Margarita, age twenty-six, holds a photograph of herself that was taken in Ukraine in 1983.

▶UKRAINE FACTS

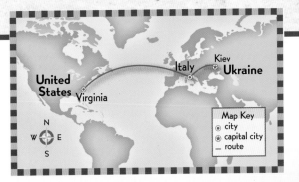

Margarita grew up in Ukraine, which was once a part of a country called the Soviet Union. The Soviet government was very strict, and people could not speak out against it. The government controlled all areas of life. For example, people could not own property. Also, they had to live in housing owned by the government.

In 1991, the Soviet Union broke into separate countries. Ukraine was one of them. Today, the people of Ukraine have more freedom than they did when the Soviet Union controlled them.

Margarita lived in Kiev, the capital city of Ukraine, before moving to the United States.

A Difficult Journey

The Ukrainian government did not make it easy for the Rozenfelds to **immigrate** to the United States. They were only allowed to take about $200 for the trip. An organization in the United States helped get permission from the United States' government for Margarita's family to enter the country and stay. The Rozenfelds were told that the journey could take anywhere from six months to a year!

Margarita and her parents took train and plane rides through several countries on their way to America. They spent three long months in Italy while they waited for permission to enter the United States. "We lived in a small basement with a cold tile floor and mice!" Margarita says.

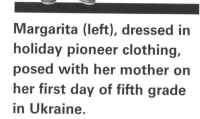

Margarita (left), dressed in holiday pioneer clothing, posed with her mother on her first day of fifth grade in Ukraine.

Margarita (right) and her best friend, who is wearing traditional Ukrainian clothing, participated in their kindergarten recital in Ukraine.

During the journey, Margarita did not go to school, she had no money, and she had no friends. "It was all very, very isolating," she says. She and her parents finally boarded a plane and headed to the United States in 1989.

A Strange New Country

Margarita's family settled in Annandale, Virginia, where Margarita's uncle and aunt lived. It was not easy at first. Margarita spent several months learning English. She also found it difficult to fit in with the other kids. Still, it was better than living in a tiny basement in Italy.

When Margarita arrived in the United States, she started sixth grade.

Margarita (front, right) enjoyed a trip to Colonial Williamsburg with her high school history class.

Margarita learned English before her parents did, which meant Margarita had to take on a lot of responsibilities at home. "I had to take care of all the bills and all the insurance forms. Any time there was a problem that required English, I took care of it. It was me, at twelve." Margarita made the best of her situation. After mastering English, she made friends and did well in school. Eventually, she went on to college and graduated in 1998.

Margarita, shown here with Ambassador Cregan, attended his Fourth of July party during her college internship in Honduras.

Margarita, posed with her father, celebrated her graduation from James Madison University with her parents.

Margarita's Life Today

What does Margarita think about her experiences today? She says, "Sometimes life throws things at you. Sometimes it makes you mad and frustrated, but usually these experiences get you to a wonderful new place. My immigration has given me such a gift."

At her job, Margarita teaches people how to succeed at work and in their personal lives.

Today, Margarita's job allows her to use this gift to help other people. She is a Life Coach, which means that she helps other people through difficult times. "I help people transform challenges into opportunities."

Margarita and her parents traveled to Mexico in 2001.

9

Hector Grillone

Hector had a happy childhood surrounded by family and friends in Argentina. He and his family were active in their church and community. Even though they lived well, Hector's father dreamed of moving to the United States where he heard that "the streets were paved with gold."

Hector's parents believed he and his brother would have more opportunities in America. They sold everything they owned and paid all their debts. Taking only one hundred dollars and four suitcases, Hector and his family boarded a small airplane. They left Argentina for the United States when Hector was six years old. "I remember being both excited and scared," says Hector. "We didn't know anybody, and we were leaving all of our relatives."

Hector, age fifty, holds a photograph of himself that was taken in Argentina in 1958.

ARGENTINA FACTS

Hector was born in 1953, during Juan Perón's rule. This Argentinian president was known for his strict form of government. Under Perón's rule, there was no freedom of speech. People who spoke out against the government were punished. Argentina's economy suffered, and people grew unhappy with the government. Perón was thrown out of power in 1955. Since Perón's rule, the people of Argentina have gained more freedoms. However, the country is still working to build a stable government and **economy**.

Before moving to the United States, Hector stayed with relatives in Buenos Aires, the capital of Argentina.

Hector (second from right) posed with his parents and his brother Daniel on the day their family left Argentina.

A New Home

The Grillones moved to Santa Monica, California, in June 1960. Hector spent the first summer adjusting to his new home and making friends. He was amazed by how different everything was. "The root beer tasted exactly like a kind of medicine in Argentina," says Hector.

Hector, who had been too young to attend school in Argentina, started first grade. Learning English was a challenge for him and his family. Hector's teacher was very helpful. Still, the language **barrier** made school difficult. "I remember coming home crying because I couldn't speak the language. I wanted to learn so badly," says Hector. Hector and his parents learned English by reading and by watching television. In just three months, Hector was fluent in English.

Hector (left) and his family were very excited when they purchased their first car in the United States for only $60.00.

12

Making a Difference

Hector's parents were always looking for ways to improve their lives. As a result, the Grillones moved often. In each new place, they made **contributions** to the community and the church. They also made changes to each of their homes. "We left each place better than we found it," Hector says.

Hector always strived to do better. He did well in his studies and made new friends. He participated in sports, theater, and Boy Scouts. In high school, Hector competed with his speech team and won the state championship. Over the years, the Grillones welcomed actors, politicians, and musicians into their home. Hector was comfortable with meeting new people and enjoyed learning from them.

HECTOR R GRILLONE

TROOP 279   SALT LAKE CITY UTAH

HAVING SATISFACTORILY COMPLETED THE REQUIREMENTS

IS HEREBY CERTIFIED AS AN

EAGLE SCOUT

BY THE NATIONAL COUNCIL OF THE

BOY SCOUTS OF AMERICA

DATE NOVEMBER 30 1967
590

HONORARY PRESIDENT

PRESIDENT

Hector continued through the scouting program and earned the rank of Eagle Scout when he was thirteen.

Hector competed in cross-country in high school.

13

While in college, Hector (right) and his friend Don performed their original singing and comedy act for colleges, companies, and organizations.

Hector graduated from high school in 1972 and enrolled at a college in California. He studied television production and the arts. Hector started a club to help new students adjust to college life. He was also a leader in several performing groups, including choir and theater.

In 1976, Hector's father lost his job due to the poor economy. The Grillone family decided to start a printing and graphics business. Hector worked in the family business and held several other jobs while attending college. In 1979, he received his college degree. Hector went on to work in video production for several companies. His work often required him to travel to different parts of the world.

Hector's sons often visited him on the sets of his video productions.

Hector's Life Today

In 1999, Hector moved to New Jersey with his wife and three children. Today, he is the director of video production at an educational publishing company. When not at work, Hector spends time with his family and contributes to their

Hector's family celebrated a family reunion in 2001 at Big Cottonwood Canyon in Utah.

church. He and his family enjoy Argentinian traditions, such as family barbecues called *asados* (ah-SAH-dohs) and a tea called *mate* (MAH-tay). "I am very proud of my family," he says.

Hector has learned from his experiences as both an immigrant and as a traveler. He says that people living in the United States have many opportunities that people in other countries do not have. "I've seen a lot of places that make me appreciate this country even more," Hector says.

Mate is often served in a gourd.

Hector, his wife Cory, and their children Quintin, Anders, and Sophie enjoy some time together outside of their home in New Jersey.

Marilyn Chin

When Marilyn was eight months old, her family left China for Hong Kong. In China, her family was not permitted to own property or to participate in the government. The Chins wanted a life with more freedom. Hong Kong was an improvement over China, but they wanted to keep moving. Marilyn says, "We were always looking forward to coming to America—the land of opportunity and the land of freedom."

Marilyn and her family had to wait nine long years before they could complete their journey. Family members who were already in the United States had to make **arrangements** for their immigration. The Chins had to prove that their family in the United States had enough money to support them. It took time to do all that planning and to raise enough money for the trip.

Marilyn, age forty-six, holds a photograph of herself that was taken in Hong Kong in 1962.

▶HONG KONG FACTS

When Marilyn was growing up, Hong Kong was governed by Great Britain. The British took control of Hong Kong in 1842. They gave Hong Kong back to China in 1997.

Today, Hong Kong is part of China. This urban area is famous as a trade port. Many of Asia's goods pass through it on their way to places all around the world.

When Marilyn lived in Hong Kong, ships called junks crowded the harbor near her home.

Life in America

In 1967, when Marilyn was nine, the Chins traveled to America by plane. At first they stayed at an aunt's home in Long Island. While there, Marilyn saw snow for the first time. She says, "There was so much snow that it came up to my knees. I said to myself, 'America is so beautiful!'" Later, Marilyn and her family moved to a small apartment in New York City. As the oldest, Marilyn helped her mother take care of her four siblings. Learning responsibility at a young age was a challenge for Marilyn.

Marilyn, age seven, posed with her parents and brother Robert in Hong Kong before their move to the United States.

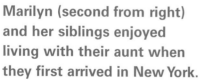

Marilyn (second from right) and her siblings enjoyed living with their aunt when they first arrived in New York.

School was also a challenge. Marilyn had always been a good student, and she expected to do well. However, she didn't speak any English, and the school she went to did little to help her out. Marilyn says of her first two years in school, "I was totally ignored in school. I couldn't understand the language, and I wouldn't say a word. The teacher let me sit in the corner and play all day. I wasn't required to learn."

Teaching Herself

By the time sixth grade started, Marilyn could speak some English, but she could not read or write. However, things finally changed that year. Marilyn says, "In sixth grade I said to myself, 'The only way I'll do well in school is to depend on myself and no one else.'" Marilyn began

At the start of eleventh grade, Marilyn began writing for her high school newspaper.

practicing reading and writing at home without the help of her teachers. Her hard work made a difference. Marilyn won an award for being the school's most improved student at the end of sixth grade.

In her teens, Marilyn continued to excel. She joined the newspaper in high school, knowing that it would force her to be a better writer. Marilyn graduated from high school with high marks and was recognized as the best student in English. After high school, Marilyn won scholarships to college and to graduate school.

Marilyn's Life Today

Since earning her master's degree, Marilyn has worked mainly in computers. She has even had the opportunity to return to Hong Kong for several years. While there, she taught computer science at a university. Returning to Hong Kong as a successful teacher was one of the most important experiences of Marilyn's life.

Marilyn is writing about her experiences in the hope she can someday share what she has learned with others.

Chin

Ya

Shung

At birth, Marilyn was given the Chinese name Chin Ya Shung (written in Chinese on left), which means "elegant moon goddess."

Today, Marilyn lives in New York City with her two sons. She likes teaching them about her native culture. Together, Marilyn and her sons celebrate Chinese holidays and enjoy homemade traditional Chinese food. She also sends her sons to Chinese language lessons.

If you ask Marilyn if she's Chinese or American, she will tell you she is a little of both. She appreciates all the opportunities that she has had in the United States but holds onto her Chinese roots. Marilyn says, "Once you manage to **overcome** a challenge, you become very strong."

Marilyn with her sons, Christopher (center) and Mathew (right), practice writing in Chinese together.

Learning From Immigrants

Every year, hundreds of thousands of people immigrate to the United States. Each has a story to tell. Margarita, Hector, and Marilyn all faced **hardships** and challenges coming to America. Yet, they all say that their experiences made them better people. They see the world from many **perspectives.** They get along with many different types of people. They strive to build on their experiences and to get the most out of life. If you listen to the stories that immigrants tell, you might be able to learn some of the things that they have learned.

Classrooms in the United States are made up of students from all over the world.

▷ BECOMING A CITIZEN

In the twentieth century, nearly 47 million people immigrated to the United States. Like the three people in this book, these people all moved to the United States permanently. They left behind their old countries for good and became U.S. citizens.

To become a U.S. citizen, immigrants have to give up all claims to citizenship of other countries. They also have to agree to obey all the laws in the United States. In return, U.S. citizens have many rights such as freedom of speech and the right to vote.

Glossary

arrangements	plans or accommodations
barrier	something that prevents a person from doing something else
contributions	something given, such as money, services, or ideas
discrimination	when someone mistreats another person because of that person's ethnicity, background, or religion
economy	the things having to do with a country's money
hardships	difficulties or challenges
immigrants	people who move to a new country
immigrate	to move to a new country
overcome	to get the better of; to defeat or master
perspectives	points of view
possessions	things that belong to a person